Super Slashers

Written by
Stephen Rickard

A long time ago, many kinds of dinosaurs lived on our planet.

Tyrannosaurus Rex

Caudipteryx

Some dinosaurs walked on two legs.

This dinosaur could walk on two legs.

Some dinosaurs walked on four legs.

This dinosaur could walk on four legs.

Einiosaurus

Plesiosaur

Some dinosaurs could swim.

This dinosaur could swim. It lived in the water.

Some dinosaurs could fly.

This dinosaur could fly. It hunted in the air.

Pteranodon

Some dinosaurs were very big.

This dinosaur was very big.

It walked on four legs.

It walked very slowly.

Brachiosaurus

Some dinosaurs could run.

This dinosaur could run.

It was not a big dinosaur. It could run very fast.

It is called a **Velociraptor**.

The Velociraptor had long, sharp claws.

The claws could tear the flesh of other animals.

People call the Velociraptor the "super slasher".

A Velociraptor claw

The super slasher could run after other dinosaurs.

It could catch them and kill them with its claws.

Maybe you have seen the super slashers in a film.